it could account for the panic

exploring temporal lobe epilepsy

poems by

Liz Whiteacre

Finishing Line Press
Georgetown, Kentucky

it could account for the panic

exploring temporal lobe epilepsy

ACKNOWLEDGMENTS

We thank the following publishers for sharing these poems, songs, and
scores with their readers, listeners, and musicians:

"It could account for the panic" & "deep breaths." *Wordgathering*, vol. 17, no.
1, 2023, https://wordgathering.com/vol17/issue1/poetry/whiteacre/.
"My Breath Is Fire," "Alone in Fear," "Deep Breaths," "It Could Account
for the Panic," "My Lifebar Glows," & "Next Season Will Be Better."
Seasons of Seizing: Six Poems on Temporal Lobe Epilepsy. Composer
Meadow Bridgham. Lyricist Liz Whiteacre. Alanala Publications, 2022.

Publisher: Leah Huete de Maines
Editor: Christen Kincaid
Cover Art: Liz Whiteacre
Author Photo: Lee Hull Moses
Cover Design: Elizabeth Maines McCleavy

Order online: www.finishinglinepress.com
also available on amazon.com

Author inquiries and mail orders:
Finishing Line Press
PO Box 1626
Georgetown, Kentucky 40324
USA

Contents

Meadow Bridgham,
thank you for sharing your story with us

"It's no use going back to yesterday, because I was a different person then."

—Alice

Alice in Wonderland
by Lewis Carroll

my breath is fire

my breath is fire
pumping blood stokes
      my veins—lungs,
      bellows—

my breath is fire
burns my palm that screens
      my exhales—fingers,
      dampeners—

my breath is fire
plumes trace exhales that stretch
      towards heaven—mouth,
      flue—

my breath is fire
heat dances from my lips in
      refracted waves—air,
      vent—

my breath is fire
capturing my attention—
capturing my attention—
my attention is
                  my breath
my attention is

    I cannot answer you

    I can't

my breath is fire
      my breath heats
            my breath blisters

my breath
        silences—

                us

I move like a specter

I move like a specter through this town
carrying traumas like they're grown
from a garden, nostalgic & green,

fresh when I close my eyes & harvest
them, these memories make me pause—

I move like a marionette through this hall
that stretches like taffy & smells sweet.
I cannot see its end, no light, no fight left.

I fly on strings of floss thin like sugar,
their tension so taut, I fear I could snap—

when I move, I am a shadow in this stairwell
that twists like putty in toddlers' hands.
I am swift & I am stealthy, but I stumble

when each step shifts out of place, unexpected,
so smooth & slick, my spectral wires hold me—

like a dancer, my limbs are led through doors
& curbs that checkpoint the path home.
this is no rhumba, but a serenade, a comfort

warm & sweet. I trust the cosmic hands
that propel me. confident I won't misstep—

I move like a catfish, bully obstacles that dissolve
like Alka-Seltzer, until my path is clear & clean.
agile & nubile, this choreography, intuited

in this dark, sonic in this dream, I'm feverish
anticipating what this might mean—

as a specter I move, deft & nimble, graced with
Serendipity's blessings, navigating this moment
on autopilot until my body & soul reconnect,

senses wake, conjoin, engage. body-mind united,
the controller unplugged, this game shut down.

can we name this?

it's living in a wintery mix, waiting on a diagnosis.
not quite rain, not snow, not hail—but I can feel it:
cold, sloppy, bone chilling. it leaves me damp when
I dodge puddles down the drive to see if
                           there's news in the mailbox.

the wait on a name feels like spring's dark leap forward,
& I fumble the routine as I ready for work, my brain still
processing half-remembered dreams, pre-dawn coffee.
I am forgetting things, distracted by the exhaustion of
                           trying to find an accurate name.

it's a pleasure sounding Latin names in the seed catalog:
zinnia violacea of the family *Asteraceae, paeonia* of the
Paeoniaceae family—but I can't locate a picture that
identifies the small green leaves that snake our grass,
                           though I know its name exists.

as sure as I know around Mother's Day the peony buds
will be near their bloom, zinnia seeds will push the soil,
unfurl lacy leaves, and the viny weed will battle new grass.
it takes patience, this discovery, & grit to endure the
                           naming, making it palpable.

down a rabbit hole

I'm not ready for an advanced search
yet, so I stick to the single-line search

    temporal lobe epilepsy

one of the terms a new doctor threw
into the air, & I decided to catch

because it's new, another rabbit hole
that promises terrain I've not traveled

yet. about 14,500,000 results in 0.48
seconds & suddenly my screen is

bright with brain scans, info graphics,
peoples' faces frozen in videos—like

the flotsam floating around Alice as
she fell down the hole. the Mayo Clinic

tells me "Some people remain aware
of what's happening" during temporal
lobe seizures, "but during more-intense
seizures, you might look awake
but be unresponsive," & I cling
to its "Your lips and hands may make
purposeless, repetitive movements"
because it knows me in its impersonal
prose. I'm compelled to follow the links,

breadcrumbs, leading me towards curious
characters quietly sharing symptoms &

stories, because "nobody talks about this—"
hours later, I massage my headache &

determine to create a new TLE forum to
find my tribe, cull meaning from moments

too bizarre to understand but on a base
level, building foundations for self-discovery.

alone in fear

I'm sitting here alone in fear.
people pass, they don't look back.
TLE, what's wrong with me?

doctors this & doctors that:
no answers, that's a fact.
say I'm sad, maybe mad,
say I'm depressed, & just a mess,
I'm not in tune with my mood.
say I misunderstood—

& I'm sitting here alone in fear.
people pass, they don't look back.
TLE, what's wrong with me?

I know depression, panic attacks,
don't tell me night terrors. take it back.
I know my body, that's a fact.
I know your warm-fuzzy déjà vu
doesn't make you freeze or pull
yourself through cationic pain—

I mirror your relaxed attitude
sitting here still as frozen food.
you can't know my interior
is wild with dreamscapes inferior
to this reality where I don't know
what's happening to me—

attack

did I just step down that step?
one pace closer to home, to safety?

      it's déjà vu my shoe setting
      its weight on linoleum.

did I just touch that banister?
catch myself from stumbling?

      it's déjà vu this exhausted hand
      gripping metal that should feel cold.

did I just push open that door?
move into this chill midnight?

      it's déjà vu this quick cut
      of scene from bright to night.

didn't I push open that door?
didn't I just step down that curb?

surely, I didn't reach to pluck that leaf?
my hand seems pressed against my lips.

      I went off script.
      I didn't just—
               I did not,
                         did I?

mixed moods

friends know when my mania phones,
remember the last time I wore them
down like sandstone, eroding their
patience like the surf on the shore.

they hide when I'm feeling manic, won't
pick up a call to listen to my diatribes.
my mania is sent directly to voicemail.

my dysphoria puts my phone on do not
disturb: I've no energy to talk or listen
—here in the doldrums, no wind in my sails.
my patience like an anchor stuck in salt.

I'm learning to lie to my therapist: fake
a steady baseline in the office, say
my course is clear, out of the tree line,
I'll make it to my destination fine.

smiley emojis, short replies, idk
keep me out of trouble—

maybe it's best I stay on do not disturb,
focus, keep my distance, appear just fine.

the highs & lows give me energy
to do something about this,
                                    maybe—

electrical storm

*

snapping like static when I shift my legs beneath winter
sheets, blue cracks in dappled dark, I sense a seizure come.
it's not achy joints or bloated sinuses. it's not quieted birds
& warm, heavy air before raindrops hit soil. it's a sucker
punch to my spine, electricity storming towards my brain,
sudden & violent like midwestern tornados.

I know it's hit my temporal lobes when I feel the funnel's eye:
everything's creepy calm, ultra-vivid, cinematic, & I hover
above myself now with the wind that I can't feel blowing,
& I see my hands press my mouth, press the lips shut so
my wind, my life force, cannot escape, leave me hollow
like my childhood ball left for seasons under a pine tree.

*

I skim Eve LaPlante's *Seized* book review, see Lewis Carroll
& TLE—pause, consider her theory that Carroll turned
some of his seizures into Alice's adventures. I marvel
at Wonderland as backdrop—hypergraphia fueling
his pen. or pencil? his commitment to communicate
his curiosities: realities forged when time stands still
& we seize, able to bridge a dimension between brain's
interior & exterior. I don't know how to explain it to you.

I fill up notebook after notebook, but I cannot find a
narrative, my Alice, my White Rabbit, my Mad Hatter.
I turn to the piano, find my moods between ascending
scales—until softness. I can rest. draw strength
from the reverberation of my score's fermata.

*

Natalie Angier reports for *The NY Times*, "Although the seizures
may be undetectable to observers, they can prompt symptoms
like hallucinations, powerful religious sensations, fury, fear, joy
and—a blessing for those in the arts—an unquenchable desire
to write or draw, a desire that persists even after the seizure is
over." & I can't help but nod. yes, those moments after when
my body burns. electrical pulses that make me weep, breathe
deeply, creating a bellow that fuels late night compositions.
I binge & purge, eating up all the oxygen in the room as I try.
I try to help you hear it, see it, feel it too, these hallucinations
as real as a comforting touch, your bosom cradling my head.

to consider my craft, my art, my music is nothing without my brain
in spasm leaves me adrift. like wandering the wreckage after
the storm, the beams chewed up & spit on the lawn, childhood
memories from albums blown across the yard, a life spilled out
for the neighborhood to gawk at as they pity the insurance claims,
the loss of resources, the interruption in schedules. I am the sum
of all my parts, & I give thanks for the storms, opportunity for
regrowth, the fertility that settles in, grows me stronger.

deep breaths

let's circle 'round to get to the point:
deep breaths pull in tangential blooms
of microscopic flowers into our lungs—
beauty breathed out. repeat.

it's simple. tune out the talking. let's cut
past the remembered trauma, sitting upstairs,
hands clasped 'round an imagined bouquet.
injected into this dream, we'll rise into nostalgic
air, blurry & warm like dandelion fuzz in the sun.

repeat the breath, blinking. let's pretend we
won't hear the vase shatter downstairs. tune out
the screaming. focus on the taste of zinnias, red & pink.
repeat. colors bubble like watercolors on wet paper.

let's circle 'round to get to the point:
focus on good feelings' bloom warm in our guts.
let's pretend they won't seize, leave us shaking,
alone on a bed in a different room

all warmth gone. still, in a cold moment—

in this silent mouth

I feel blood travel hot through capillaries
                              sense the budding
of pink blooms on tense cheeks
                                   their thorny vines
                         tracing this pale neck
           reminding me to swallow the biter lump stuck
in my throat

                         indecisive— lungs or stomach? —my
sandpaper tongue
roughs my tender palate

              which can only taste sanguine shame
              which settles like plaque in my silent mouth
              which is unable

              to shape

                   a sound

                         of defense

it could account for the panic

What if Alice woke again? Woke again with the bitter taste of shrinking potion on her tongue, and the White Rabbit beckoned once more? What if you could talk yourself out of a focal aware seizure? Did you ever think about that? Or are you thinking about that rabbit and that bitter potion and crawling elbow over elbow into a dark, gritty hole? Of being lost? Of adventure? Am I talking too much? You know, Alice had questions that never got answered and rapid heartbeats and deep breaths that soothed her confusion. Sometimes. Neophobic? Did you ever think about that? Maybe. It could account for the panic that made Alice pause. Pause and stall before chasing that white rabbit, dressed in his finest. Again. Curious. Heart beating, breath short, each detail cinematic—too much, too bright, you know? Am I talking too fast? No. No. You know, some call it a simple partial seizure. Simple. But, it's not simple, you know? When I seize—but only partially, like Alice, paused in one moment, caught in one moment—I focus on making the right choice. You know, Alice had choices. She got to choose: too big or too small, this path or that path. Curious-er. Then, curious-er. Maybe I am talking too much? But, we haven't seen each other in so long. There's so much to ask you. What if you were injected into a dream, trying to ride a dysphoric, euphoric, chaotic roller coaster, trying to follow disjointed details, forcing a narrative? Did you ever think about that? It could account for the panic that makes everyone pause. Freeze under its weight. The glow of synesthesia. What was that word? No, what did that word taste like? No, what time is it? We haven't got much time left together, do we? Because, aren't we late? Late for the terror we know is coming? Maybe in just a few moments. When a director yells "cut!" and our scene, no, my seizure, is over. Did you ever think about that? Maybe we leave the dream, like Alice, awake and shaking. Do you get it yet? I'm trying. I am really trying. You see, it's curious. When I seize— but only partially, like Alice, caught in that moment unable to tell you, precisely, what just happened—the aura starts as a buzz in the back of my head. And, I start thinking, maybe I'm on an adventure like Alice. Just paused in a moment of decision. Taking all the curiosities in. Trying to make the right choice. It could account for my panic. Did you ever think about that?

triggers

why do people look at me like that?
I'm not sure how to read them &
their innuendos. it makes my chest

feel tight, like a vice gripping my ribs,
like I can't take a breath without breaking.

why did that person touch me like that?
I'm not sure how to read them &
their innuendos. it makes my blood

feel hot, like lava pumping in my veins,
like I can't touch flesh without breaking.

why did that person tell me like that?
I'm not sure how to read them &
their innuendos. it makes my head

throb, like beats pumping in my brain,
like I can't think without breaking.

anxiety has me replaying each moment
on slow motion, I can't tell if people
are serious. it's like standing at a podium

every eye scrutinizing my body & soul.
I'm not sure how to act, if they're saying

false facts—it makes my stomach retch,
like seeing a squirrel dead in the road,
like I can't make a move without breaking.

I'm not sure how to read people & their
innuendos. *why'd they have to do that?*

my lifebar glows

I'm exhausted from hours of uneasy scales.
need time to unwind, time to inhale

& exhale, but time blurs, tightens my gut.
fuzz in the back of my skull—static like I forgot.

it's sharp like I panicked, hollow like I forgot lunch.
blood drains from fingertips, I can't feel my touch.

my arms swing like pendulums, propelling
me down a lengthening hallway, quarrelling

with my shadowself, limbs akimbo,
squinting down the hall's vertigo effect.

it's like I'm watching myself on video,
my body doing things I didn't tell it to.
flash of a load screen, I'm pixelated.
I'm a player in a game, manipulated.

my lifebar glows: my palm presses my hot air in.
until midnight's frost wakes me, cold against my skin.

my routine's familiar. I lower my cold hand,
gently, feel the night particles, unplanned.

the rough of my jeans, as I locate my keys,
brings me back, back home to you.

resolution

damn, if I didn't find myself missing the aura,
like unexpected love notes from you, which make
me warm, a little giddy, knowing I am unique, that

something will happen—soon—to break up
the monotony, like your laugh, your kiss,
your sleepy curves under the covers at dawn.

double time heartbeat, groove before my breath
catches & I disassociate, lucid dreams guiding
my moment. a director who makes me feel safe.

in these foggy panoramic waking dreams when
I can see patterns like shamans on shrooms,
when details are etched on imaginary windowpanes,

when, Euphoria blows gently on my neck—I crave
the moment before waking, when my brain captures
electrical impulses I want to whisper to you.

it's like the gentle period when our breaths syncopate
unfettered by what's about to happen. I keep resolving
to follow the protocols to keep the seizures at bay, but

damn, if I don't find myself missing the fevered
productivity before a crash: my secret worry is that TLE
might be my superpower, the muse to my art, my love.

if you remind me to take my medication, I promise I have.
I commit to lifestyle changes, to keep me, us, even keeled.
if you ask how I am (I am ready to welcome the next flush).

next season will be better

I didn't want to jinx it, but I did over coffee
commenting on all the seasons since I've seized.
like our garden, Life's been growing in coordinated
rows: blooms & harvests timed with sun sets.

on the horizon I see storms coming, flash floods,
hail. triggers, like lightening, could signal failure—
I worry over signs like powdery mildew & fungus.
things peck me like aphids, puncturing my nerves.

you're my ladybird: protector, you hold me together.
we'll pull things up, start over: next season will be better.

you were in the bedroom making routine sounds,
& I smelled peonies on the table, signaling the end
of another day. dirt under my fingernails seemed stark
before I pressed my hands against my mouth.

sounds slowed, I warmed, & the porch light dimmed.
I couldn't hear your call, only my heart drumming
like the thrum of gasoline mowers & blowers.
heartache—like finding that deer stomped the melons,

cabbage moths devoured crops, or blight-blanketed
roses—deep in my chest until I curl next to you.
I can live with seizures, with you. I'll learn the clues,
read soil & weather, prepare for ever.

you're my ladybird: protector, you hold me together.
with you, I'm stronger, I want to work towards our harvest.

we'll pull things up & start over: next season will be better.
we'll learn from this, grow, & move on.

about the poems
by Meadow Brigham

When I was in middle school, I spent the night at my eldest sister's house. I brought with me my cheap, plastic electric piano. I balanced it on the small desk in front of her computer and logged on to the now-defunct website, "Charlie's Piano." This was in the days before social media and IMSLP.

I was self-taught and getting decent at sight-reading. I read Beethoven's "Waldstein" Sonata for the first time that night. I remember being baffled by the first and second pages; it starts in C major and shifts suddenly to E major. All those accidentals excited me. What came next would be the first of many bizarre attacks.

My breath grew warm. I became nervous about something outside, anxiously pacing about from fear and confusion. Then I was struck by a vision. The world felt strange, as if I had been transported into a dream. At first, I was overcome with euphoria. I felt as if I had finally remembered something I had forgotten years prior. It felt like an intense déjà vu. But then everything changed. I heard voices. I saw lights. The room appeared to grow larger and smaller at the same time. In only a minute's time, I was left fearful on the couch with my hand over my mouth.

In 2021, I worked with Indiana poet, Liz Whiteacre, to turn my Temporal Lobe Epilepsy (TLE) testimonials into a set of poems. I set six to music: "Seasons of Seizing: Six Poems on Temporal Lobe Epilepsy," which were performed by Andrew Durham and myself on my DMA recital in November 2022 at Yale University.

Meadow Bridgham makes new music from old ideas—a kind of musical upcycling, an antique restoration. Recent appearances of their music include the Rivera Court at the Detroit Institute of Arts, the Utzon Room at Sydney Opera House, and Merkin Hall at New York's Kaufman Music Center. Meadow holds a Doctor of Musical Arts degree from the Yale School of Music, where their Violin Sonata was awarded the Frances E. Osborne Kellogg Memorial Prize for best composition written in a contrapuntal style. Learn about their music at *https://bridghammusic.com/*.

resources

Angier, Natalie. "In the Temporal Lobes, Seizures and Creativity."
  The New York Times, 12 Oct. 1993, https://www.nytimes.
  com/1993/10/12/science/in-the-temporal-lobes-seizures-
  and-creativity.html.

"Epilepsy: Simple Focal Seizure." *YouTube*, uploaded by Epilepsy
  Society, 21 May 2012, https://www.youtube.com/
  watch?v=X3_pv6us8A0.

"Focal Onset Aware Seizures (Simple Partial Seizures)." *The
  Epilepsy Foundation*, 2023, https://www.epilepsy.com/
  learn/types-seizures/focal-onset-aware-seizures-aka-simple-
  partial-seizures.

"Interview #1: Janice Coffey (Focal Onset Aware Seizures)."
  YouTube, uploaded by The Universal Design Project, 19 Aug
  2017, https://www.youtube.com/watch?v=vUADNzkIgr0.

LaPlante, Eve. *Seized*. Harpercollins, 1993.

r/TLE Group. *Reddit*, created 14 Oct. 2016, https://www.reddit.
  com/r/tle/.

"Temporal Lobe Seizure." *The Mayo Clinic*, 2023, https://www.
  mayoclinic.org/diseases-conditions/temporal-lobe-seizure/
  symptoms-causes/syc-20378214.

"Temporal Lobe Seizure." *YouTube*, uploaded by Angela McGinnis,
  31 Oct. 2015, https://www.youtube.com/watch?v=veInfvb-
  cEs.

Liz Whiteacre's poetry explores accident, disability, aging, and wellness. She is the author of *Hit the Ground* (Finishing Line Press, 2013), and her poems have appeared in *Wordgathering, Disability Studies Quarterly, Kaleidoscope, Breath & Shadow, Flying Island,* and other publications. Whiteacre is an associate professor of English at the University of Indianapolis. She teaches writing and publishing there, as well as advises Etchings Press.

www.ingramcontent.com/pod-product-compliance
Lightning Source LLC
Chambersburg PA
CBHW022108080426
42734CB00009B/1515